# Decorative Alphabets

## for Needleworkers, Craftsmen & Artists

Edited by
Carol Belanger Grafton

DOVER PUBLICATIONS, INC., NEW YORK

Published in Canada by General Publishing Company, Ltd., 30 Lesmill Road, Don Mills, Toronto, Ontario.
Published in the United Kingdom by Constable and Company, Ltd.

*Decorative Alphabets for Needleworkers, Craftsmen and Artists* is a new work, first published by Dover Publications, Inc., in 1981. The various sources for the illustrations are indicated in the Publisher's Note.

DOVER *Pictorial Archive* SERIES

*International Standard Book Number: 0-486-24175-0*
*Library of Congress Catalog Card Number: 81-66590*

Manufactured in the United States of America
Dover Publications, Inc.
31 East 2nd Street
Mineola, N.Y. 11501

# PUBLISHER'S NOTE

The history of decorative alphabets began with the ornamentation of handwritten and, later, printed books, in which decorative letters played an integral part as the initial letters of chapters, paragraphs and headings, with the largest letters making the most important textual divisions. Although printers and book designers no longer make extensive use of decorative letters, letters of this kind are still effectively employed to create striking advertisements and cover designs. In media other than printing, however, the use of decorative letters is increasing, and it is principally for the creative needleworker, craftsman and artist, whose applications of decorative alphabets are limited only by the imagination, that this volume is intended.

Graphic designer Carol Belanger Grafton has gathered over two thousand letters, including seventy-nine complete alphabets, many from rare sources that have long been out of print, and all copyright free. The volume also reflects the keen eye of Dover Publications' former needlecraft specialist, Rita Weiss, who participated in the final selection. Needleworkers may wish to make use of any number of lacy, elegant shapes (see, for example, pages 4, 6 and 7); some of the letter designs included were originally created as transfer patterns. But they will also find many styles ideally suited for needlepoint, embroidery, cross stitch and latch hooking that were first conceived for other purposes. Woodcraftsmen may choose to carve, or burn in with an electric pen, the dot letters on page 11 or the bolder shapes found on page 34. Some of the extremely elaborate alphabets, like the one beginning on page 81, will inspire artists interested in the free play of abstract shapes.

Most of the letters and alphabets in this volume were derived from the following sources:

*Alphabets, Monograms, Initials, & Crests.* New York: F. W. Bullinger, n.d.

*Artistic Alphabets for Marking and Engrossing.* New York: Butterick, 1897.

Bergling, J. M. *Art Monograms and Lettering for the Use of Engravers, Artists, Designers, and Art Workmen.* Chicago: J. M. Bergling, 1914.

Brown, Frank Chouteau. *Letters & Lettering: A Treatise with 200 Examples.* Boston: Bates & Guild, 1921.

Delamotte, F. *The Book of Ornamental Alphabets, Ancient and Mediaeval, from the Eighth Century, with Numerals.* London: C. Prang, 1916.

Esser, Hermann. *Draughtsman's Alphabets.* New York: Keuffer and Esser, 1877.

*Henderson's Sign Painter.* Newark, N.J.: R. Henderson, 1906.

Hollister, Paul. *American Alphabets.* New York, 1930.

Lindegren, Erik. *ABC of Lettering and Printing Types*, Vol. B. New York: Museum Books, 1960.

*The Real Pen-Work Self-Instructor in Penmanship.* Pittsfield, Mass.: Knowles & Maxim, 1881.

Stevens, Thomas Wood. *Lettering.* New York: Prang, 1916.

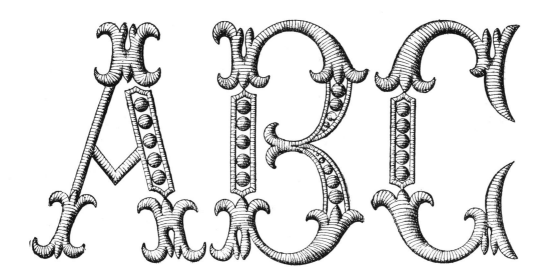

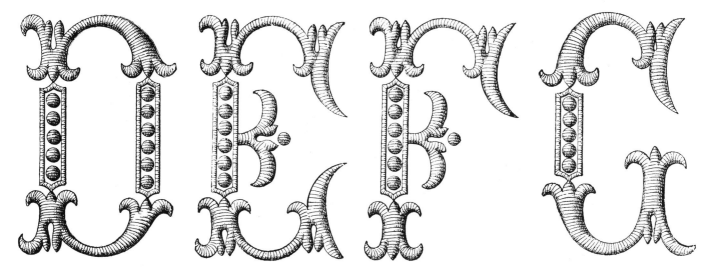

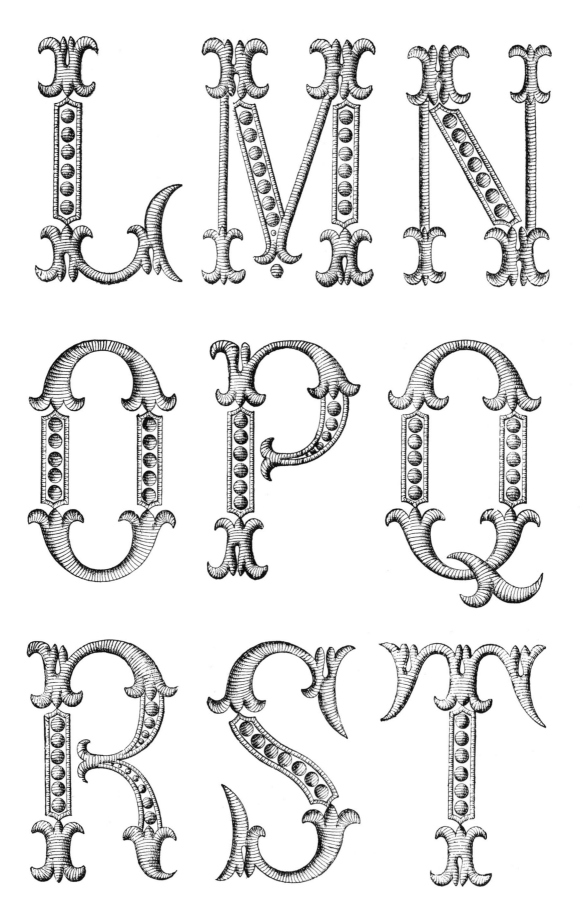

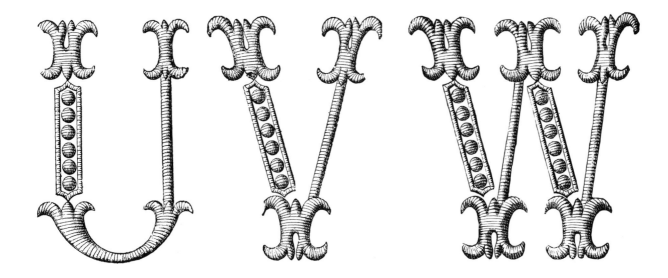

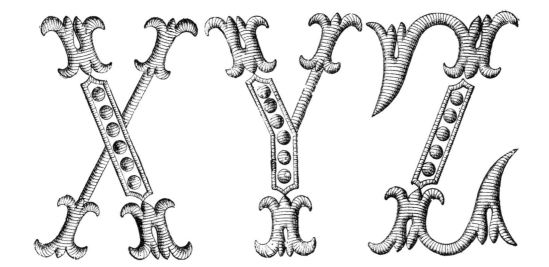

 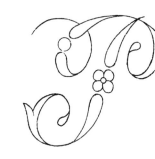 

   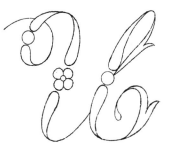

  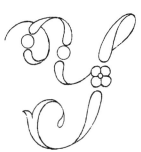

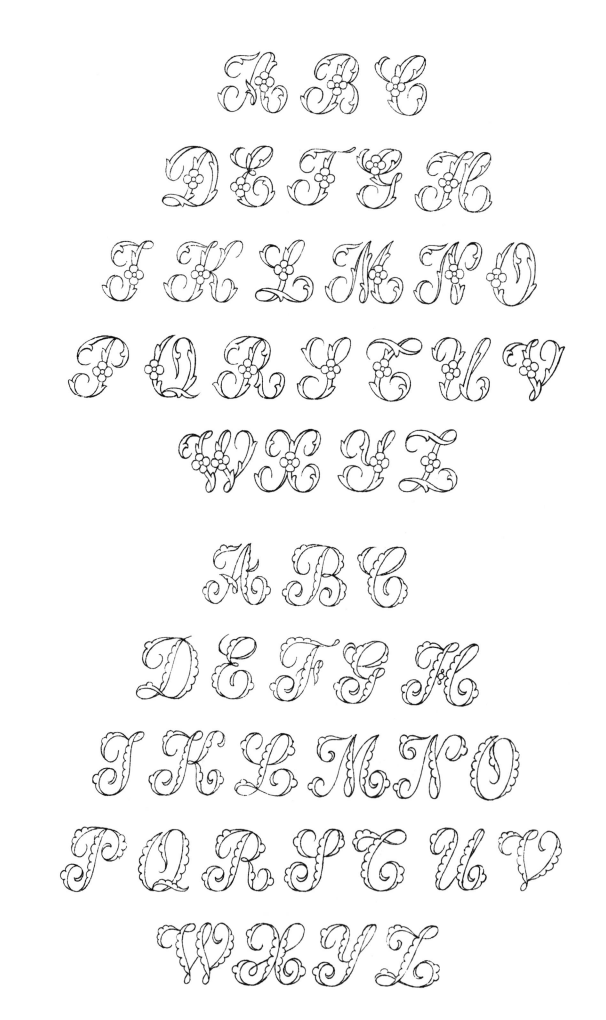

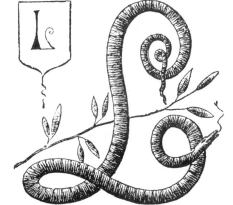

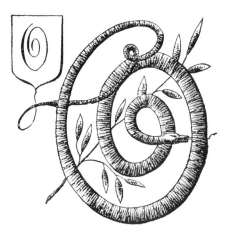
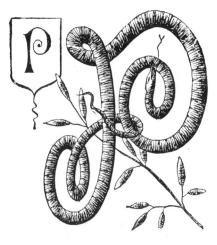

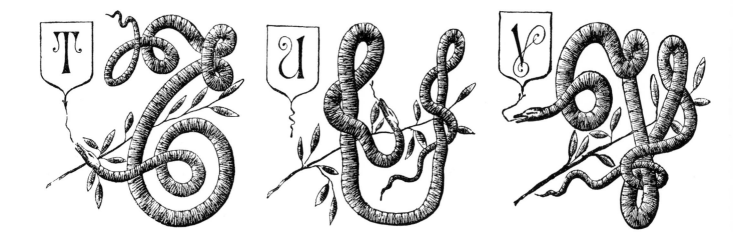

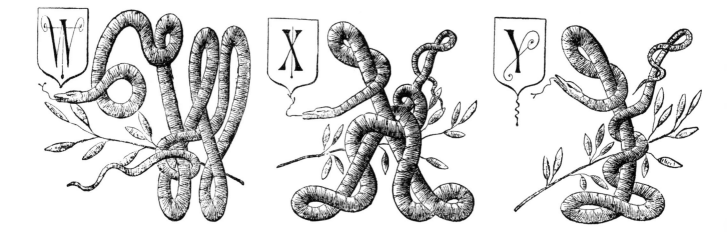

ABC

DEFGH

IJKLMNOP

QRSTU

VWXY

Z

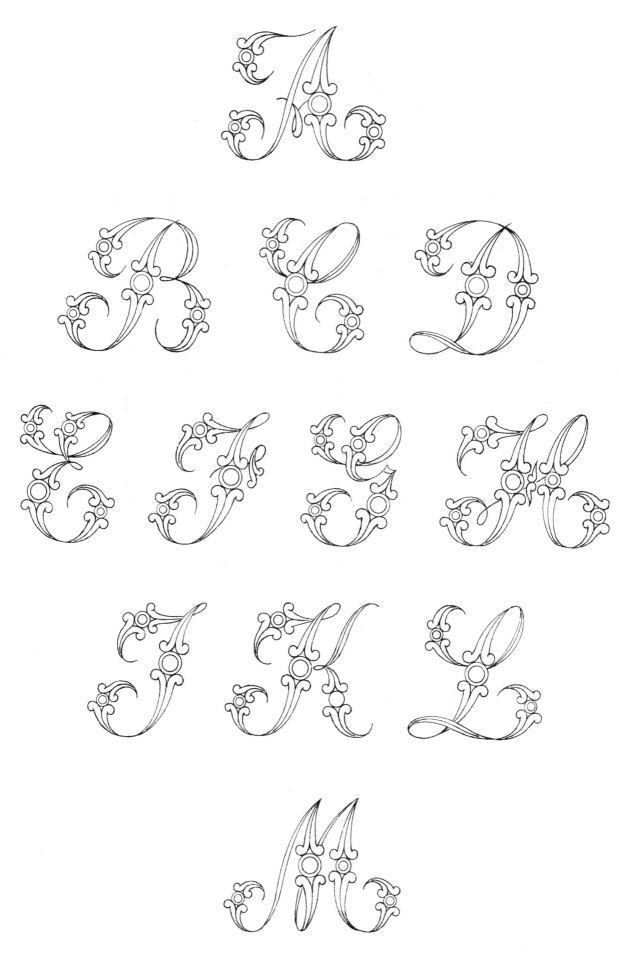

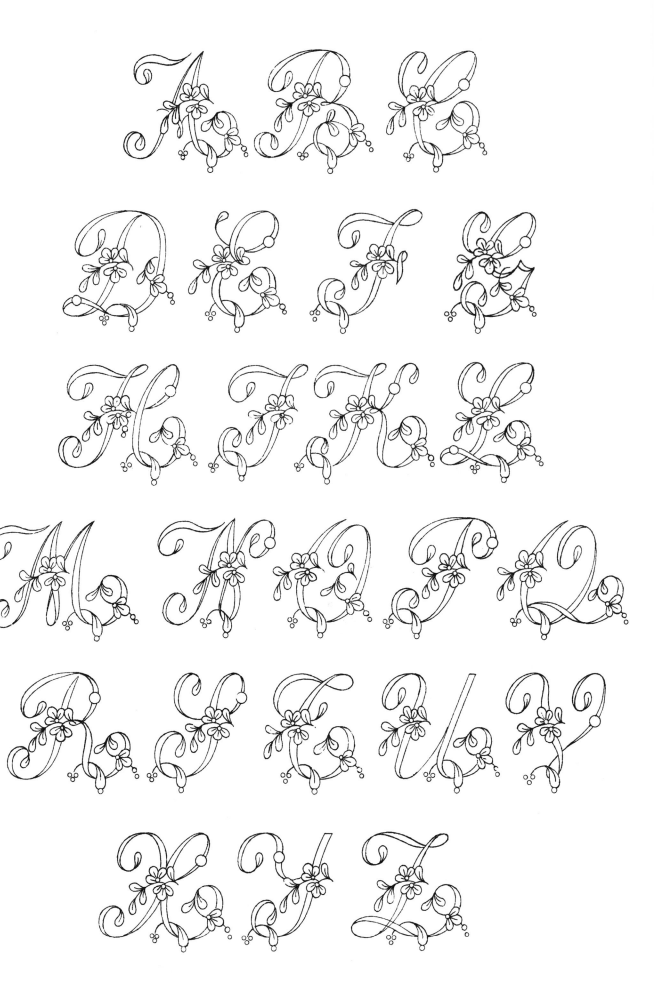

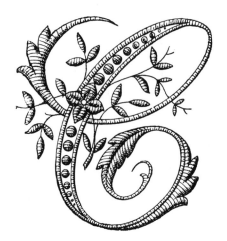

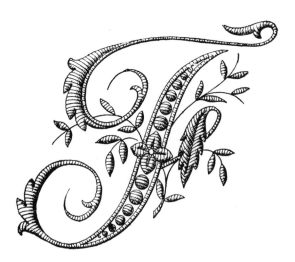

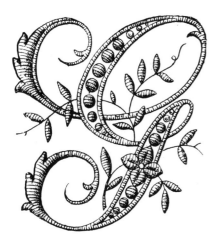

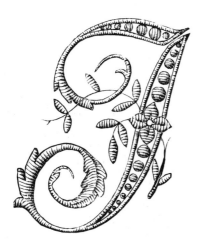

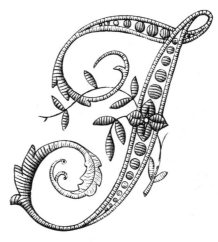

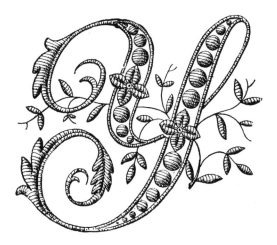

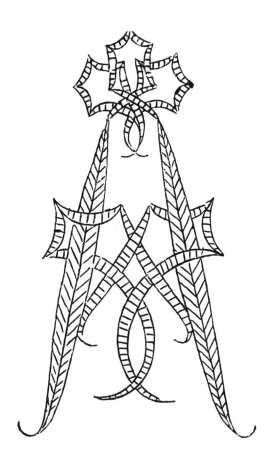

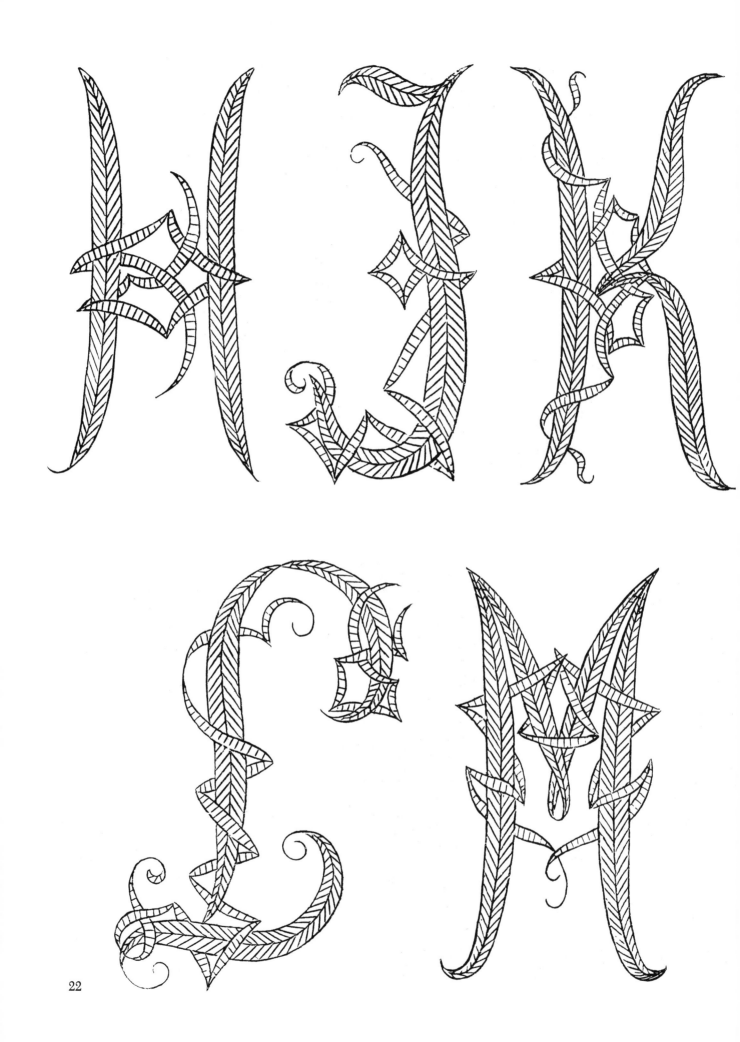

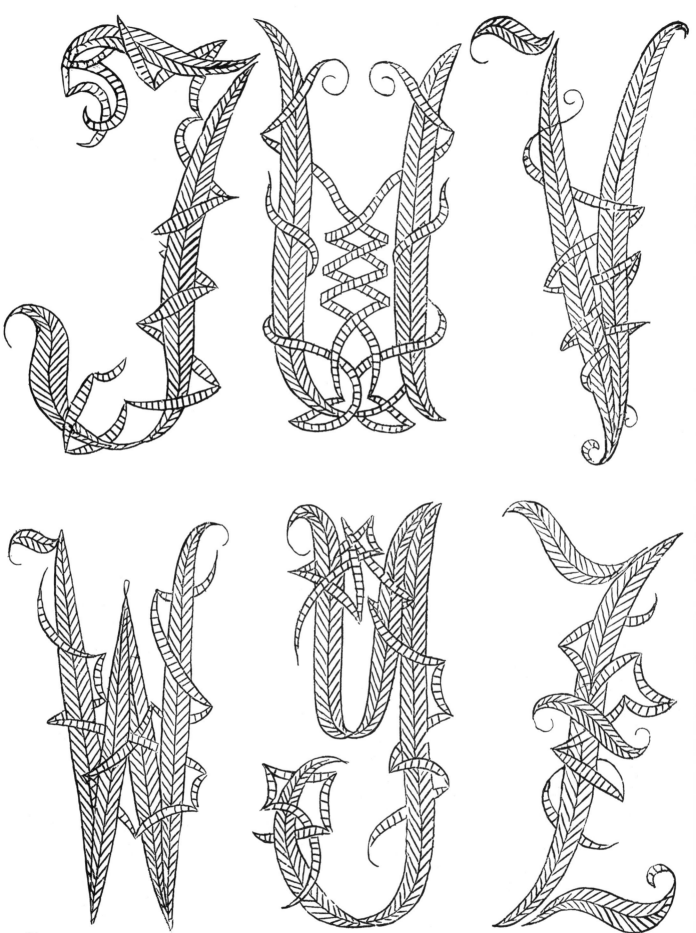

24

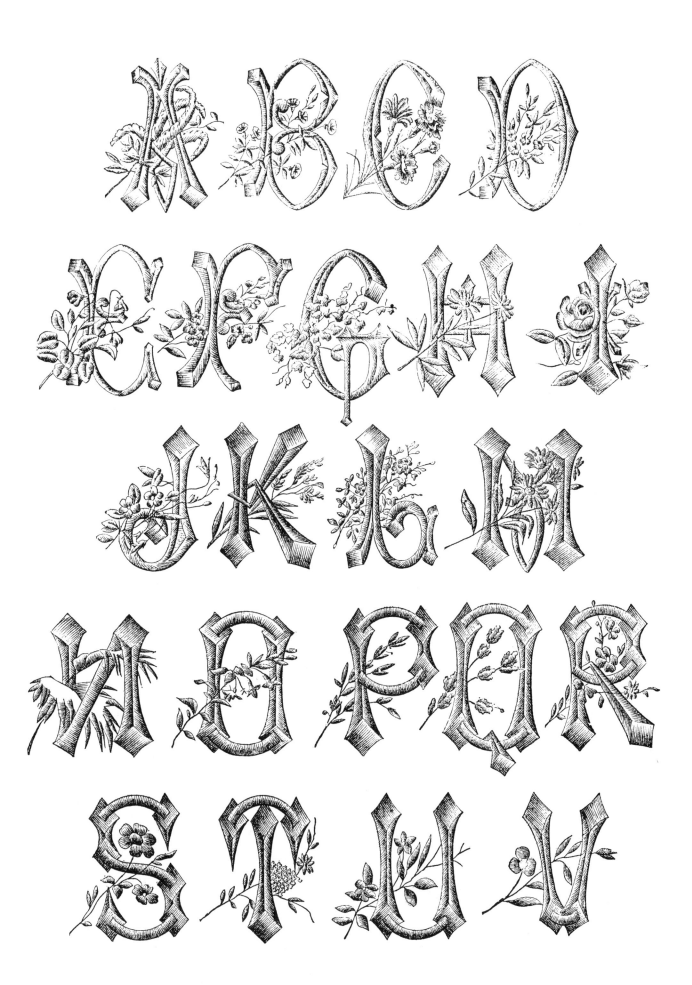

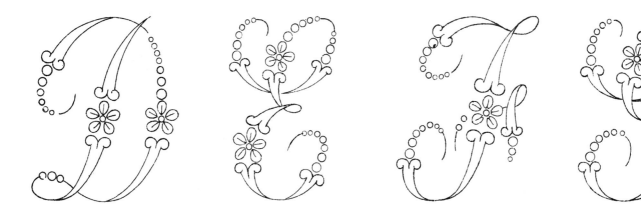

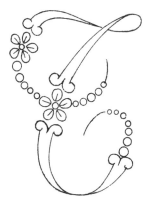

28

31

32

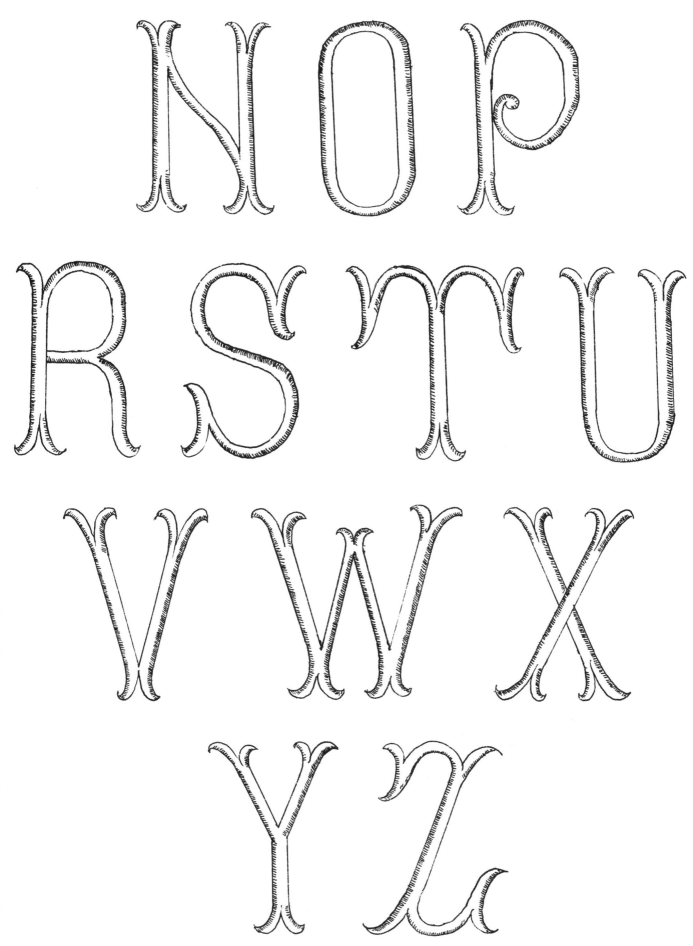

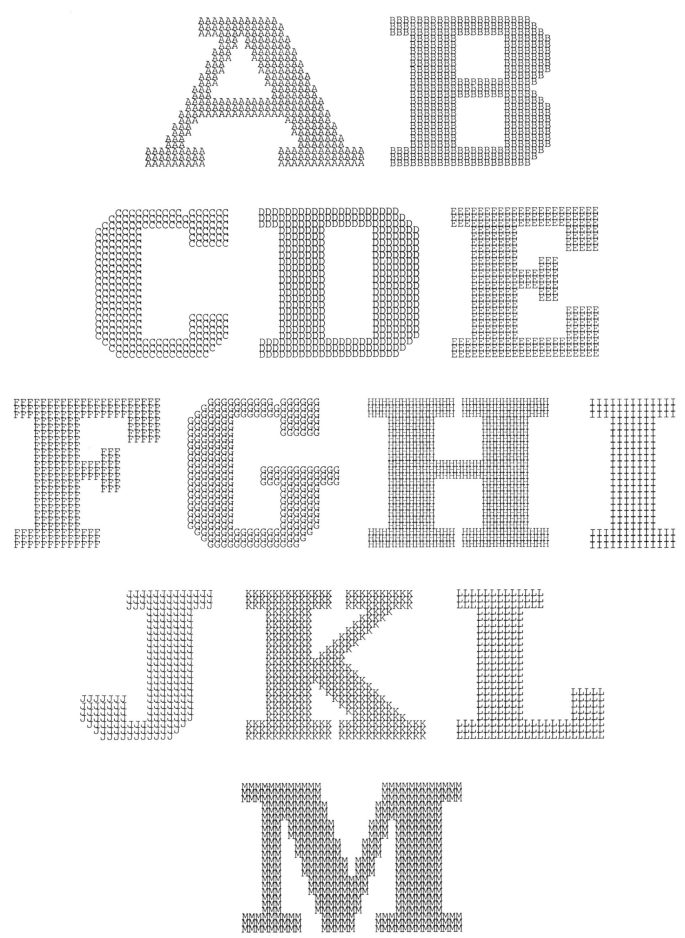

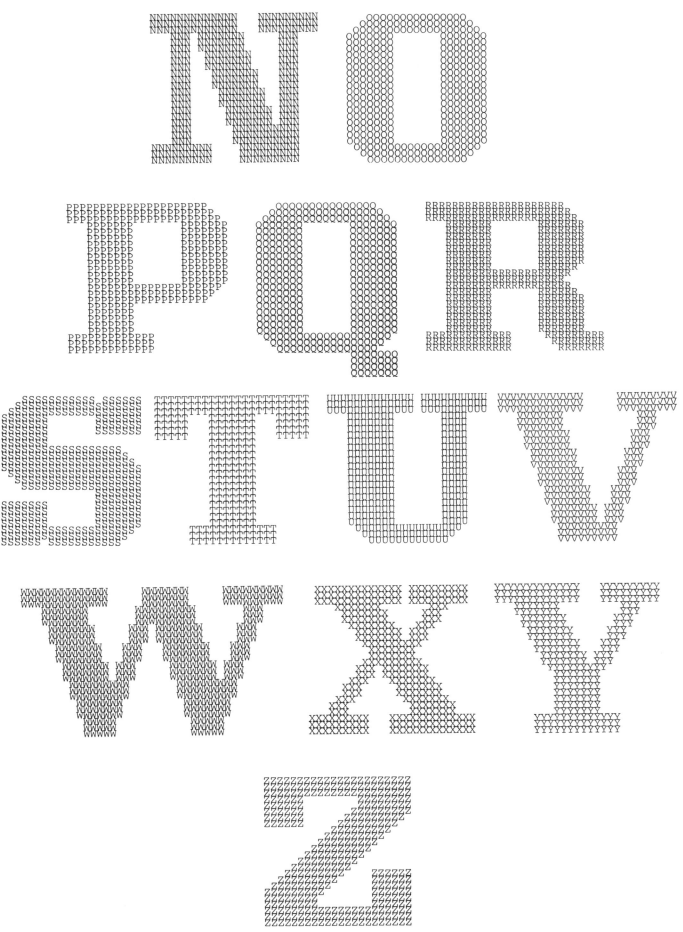

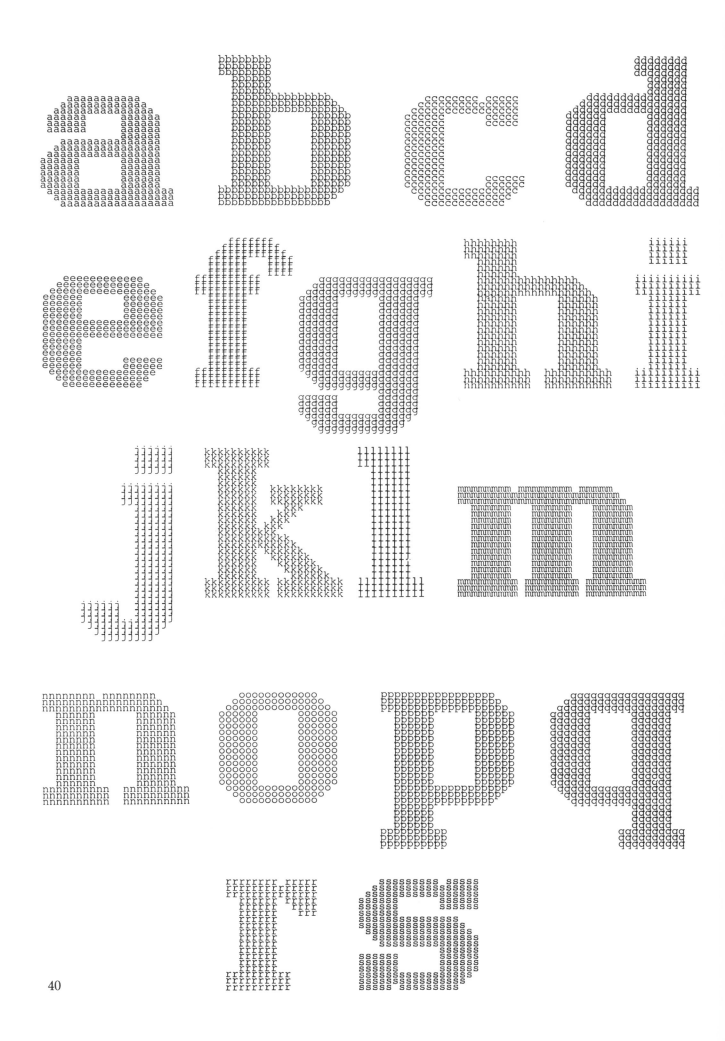

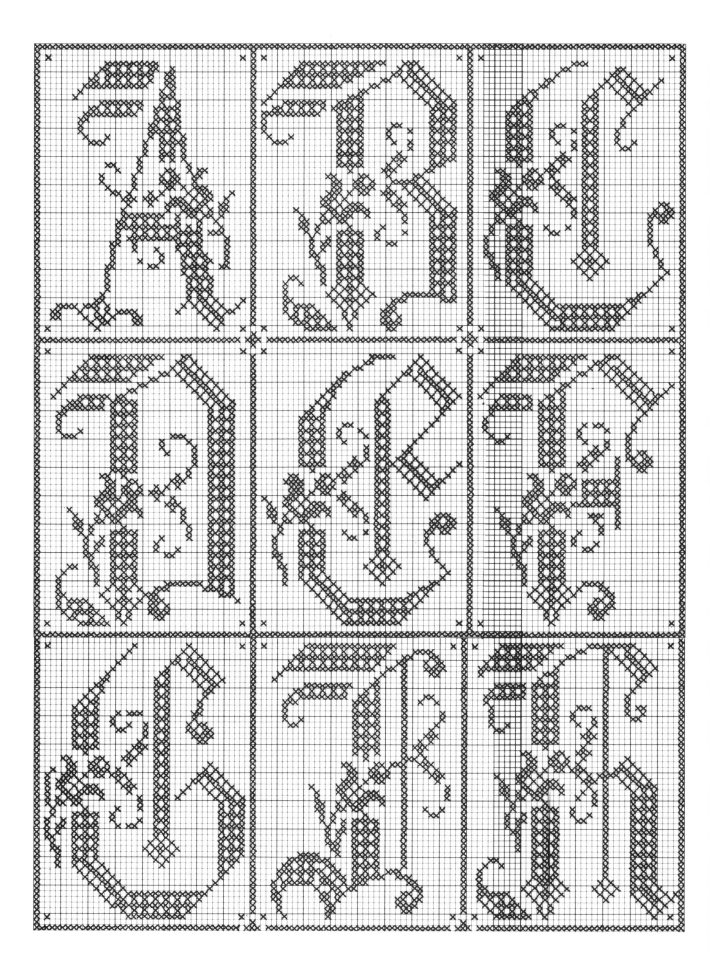

42

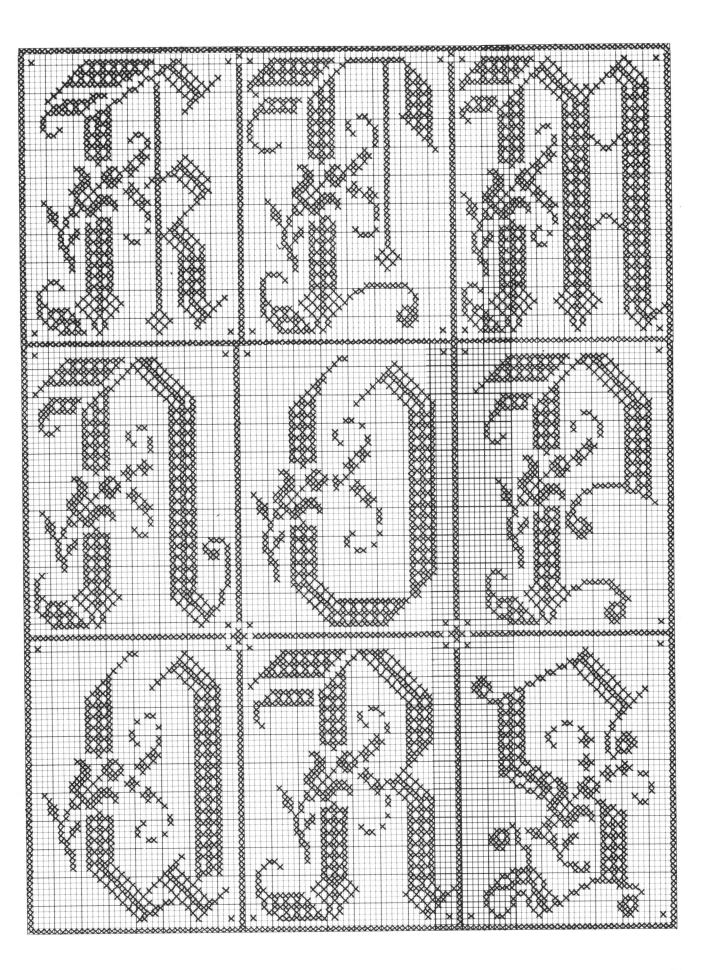

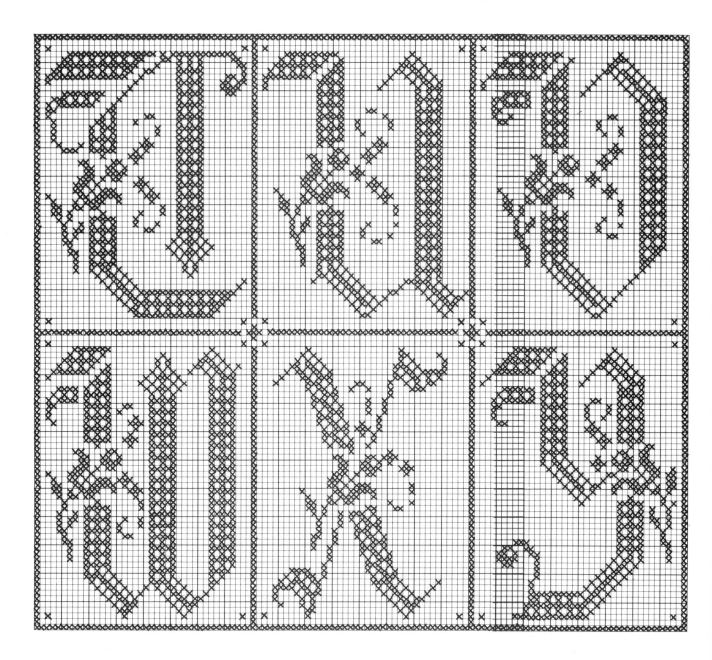

44

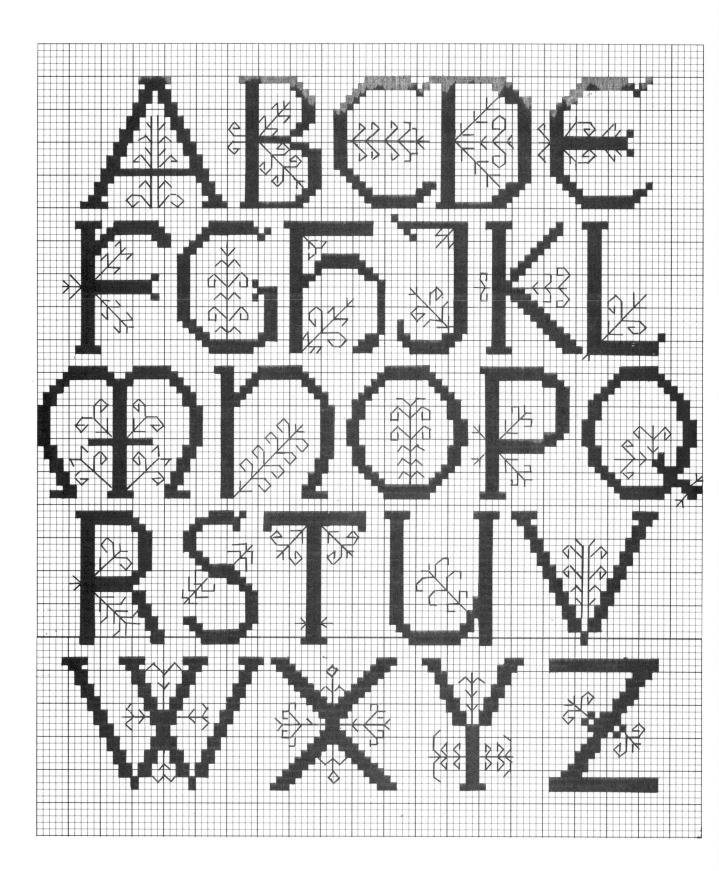

48

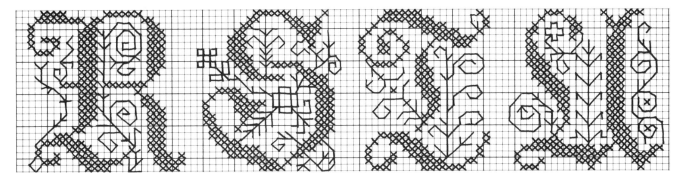

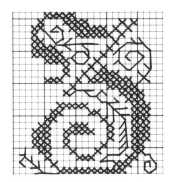

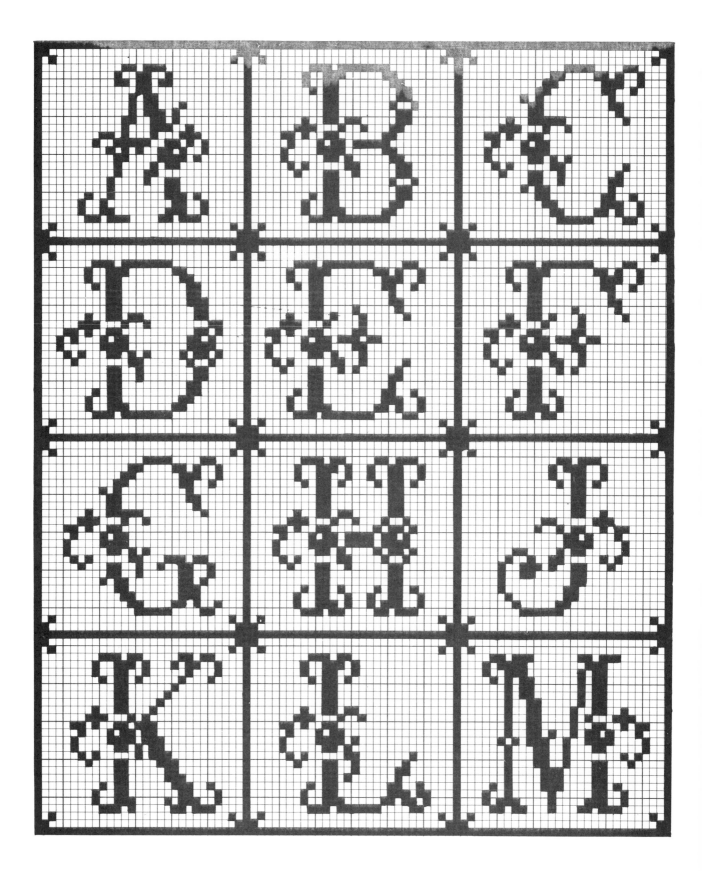

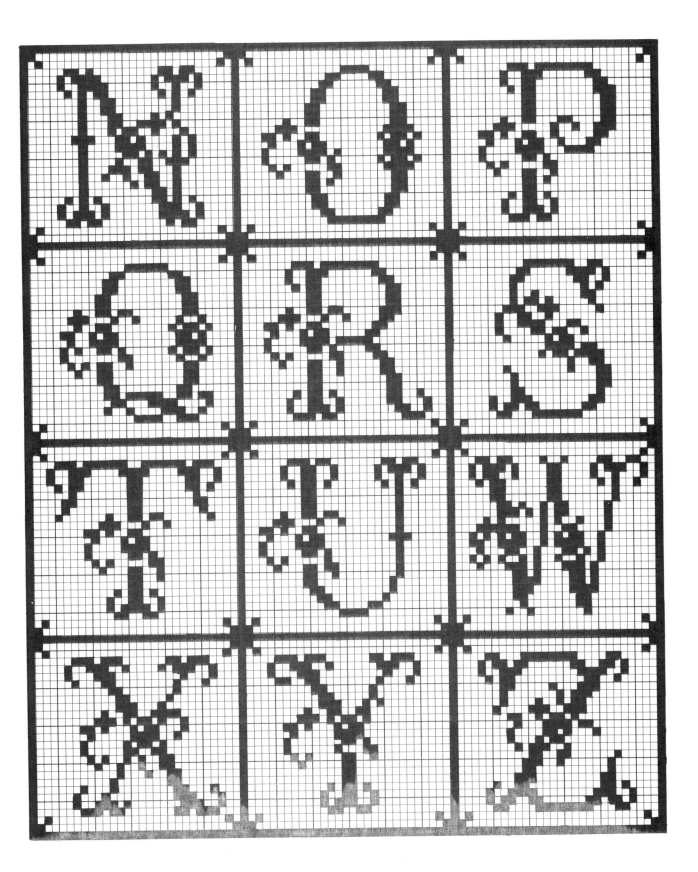

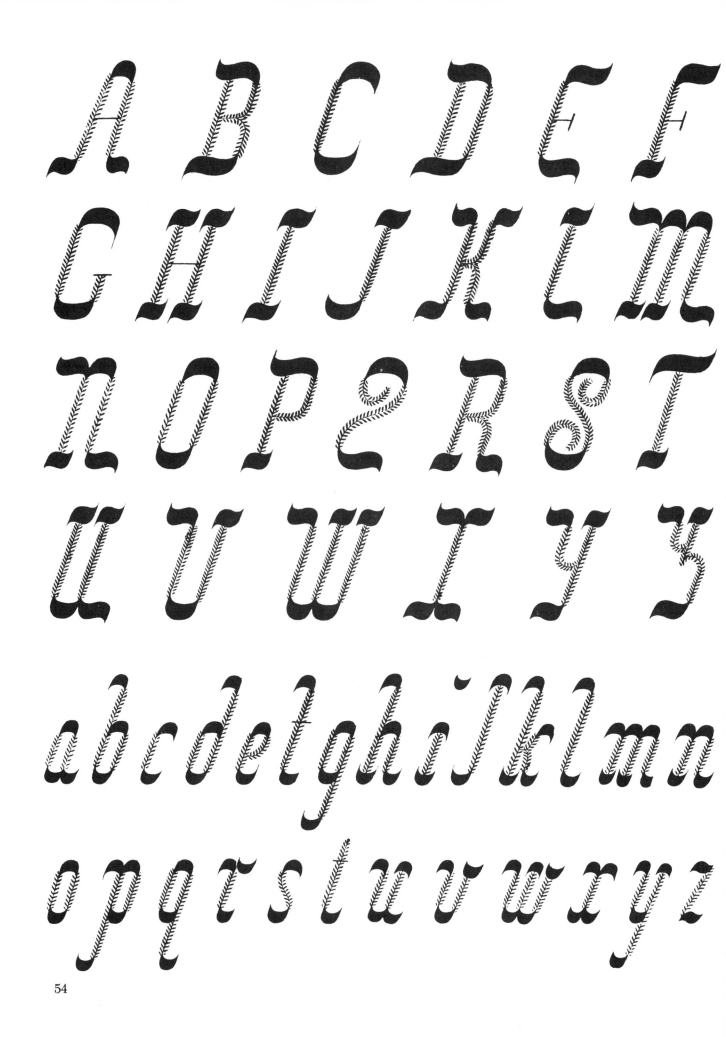

54

59

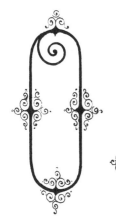

61

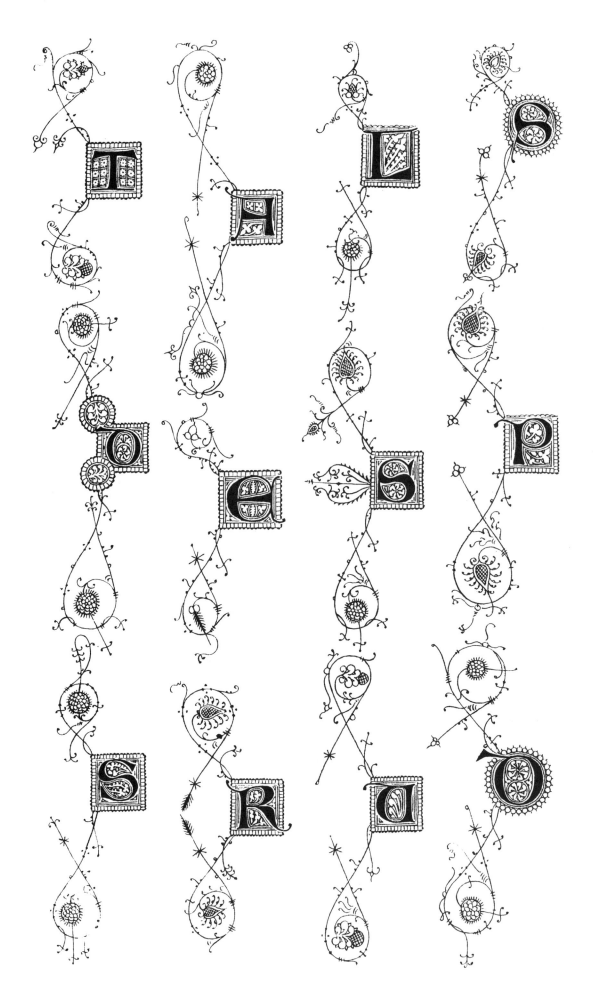

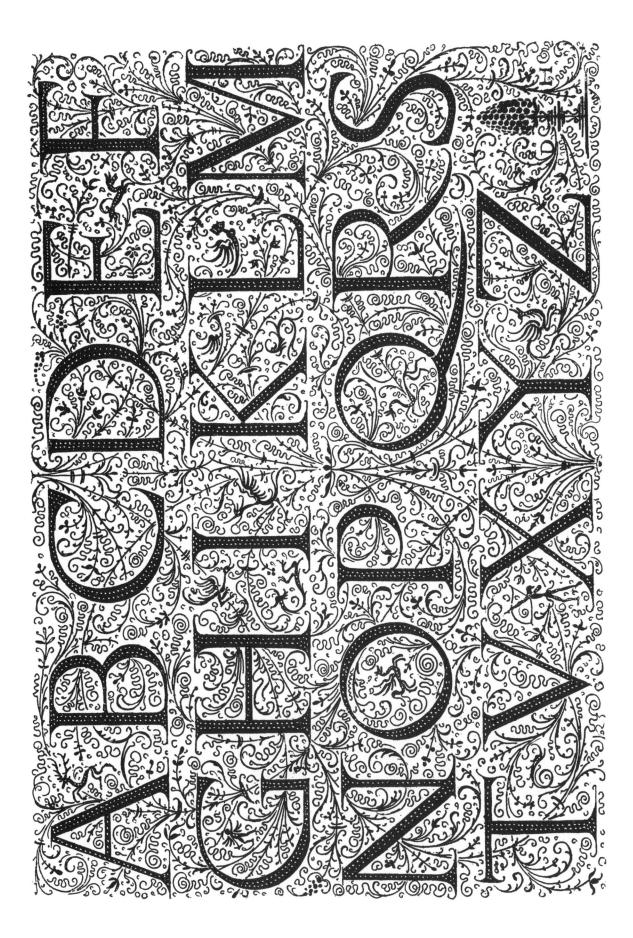

71

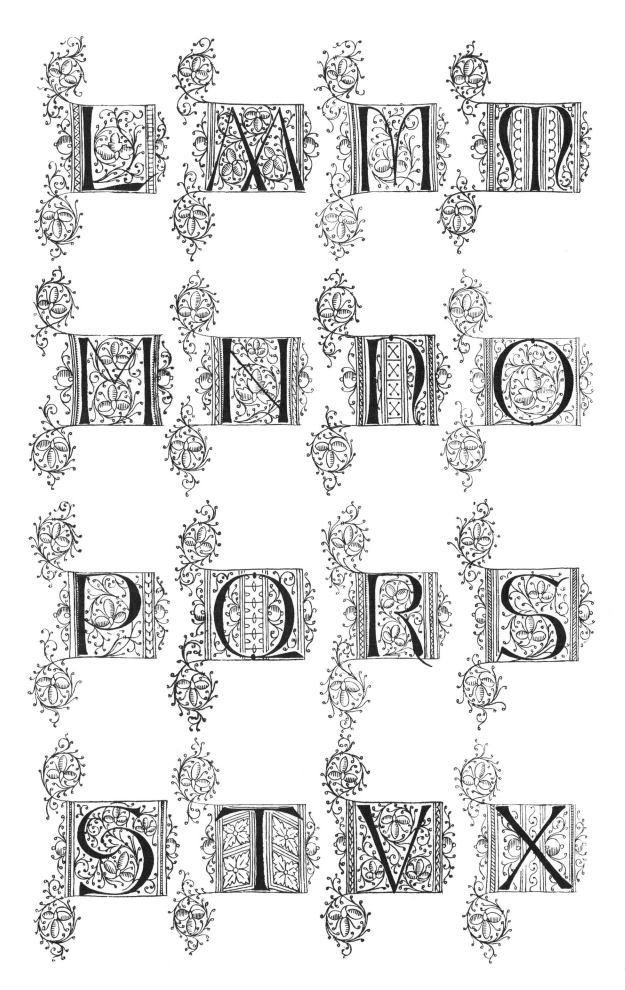

ABC
DEFGHIK
LMNOPQR
STUVWYZ

ABC
DEFGH
IJKLYNOPQR
STUVWXYH

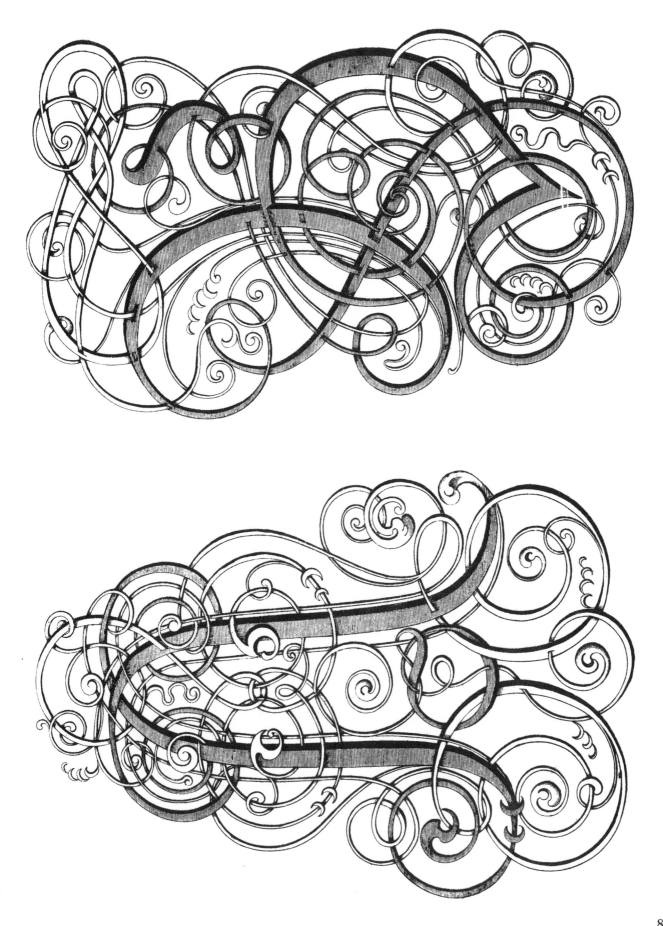

82

84

85

89

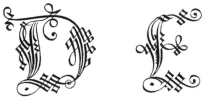

abcdeefg
hijklmmnop
qrsstuvwxyz

— 1234567890 —

ABCCDEEFCGH
IJKLCMNOPQRS
STGUVWXYZ

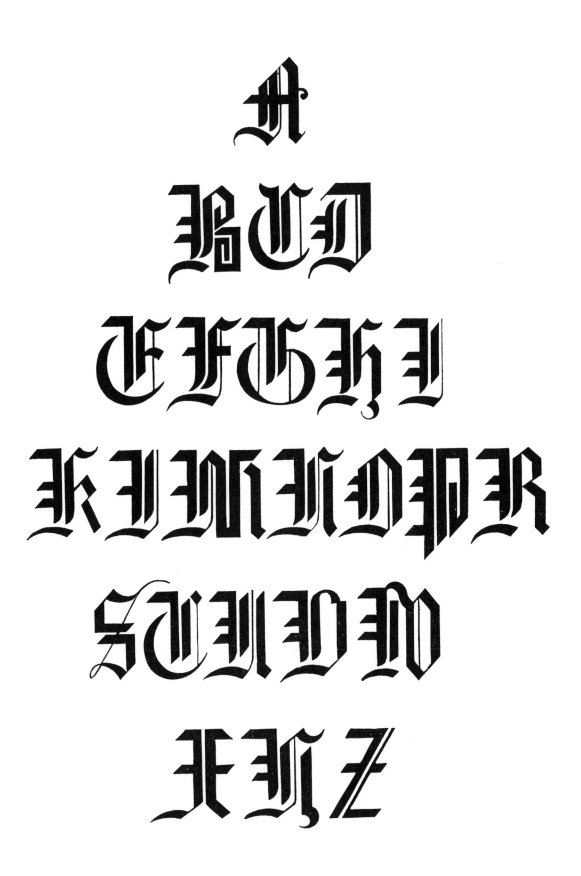

ABC
DEFGH
IJKLMN
OPQRST
UVWXYZ
&

abcdefghijklmnopqrstuvwxyz

1234567890

104

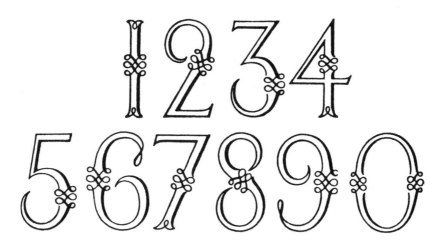

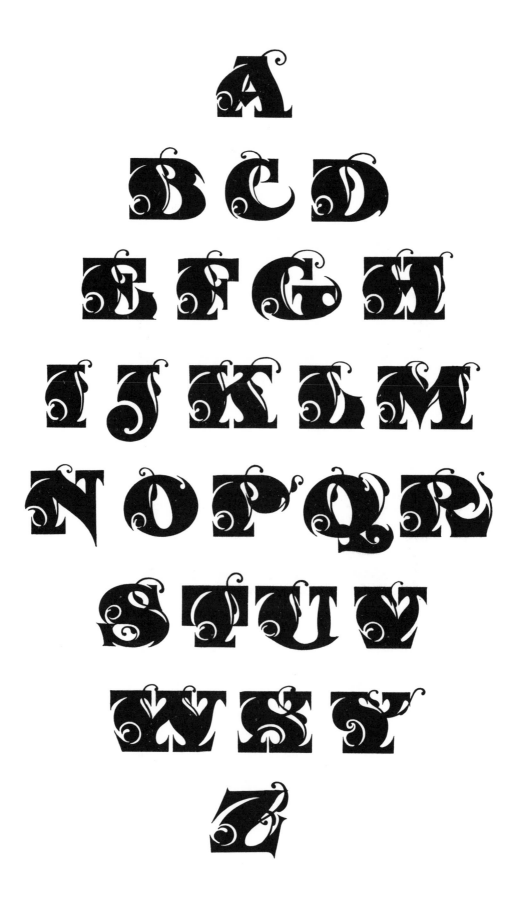

abcdef
ghijklnmopqr
stuvwxyz

abcdef
ghijklmnopqrſ
sktuvwxyz

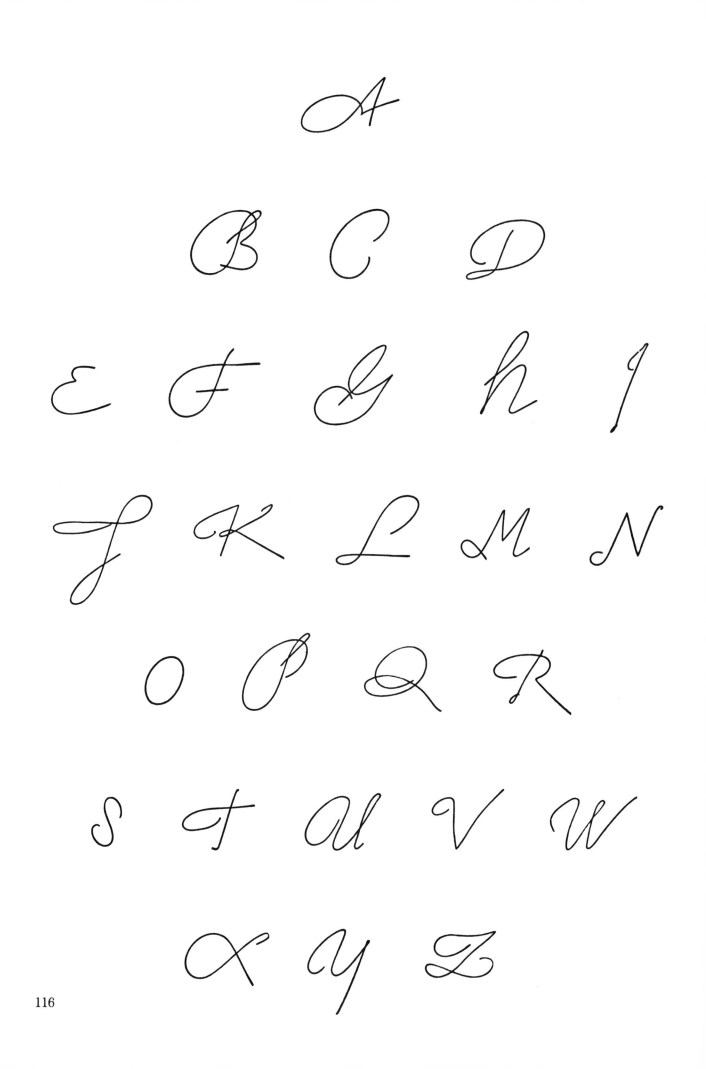

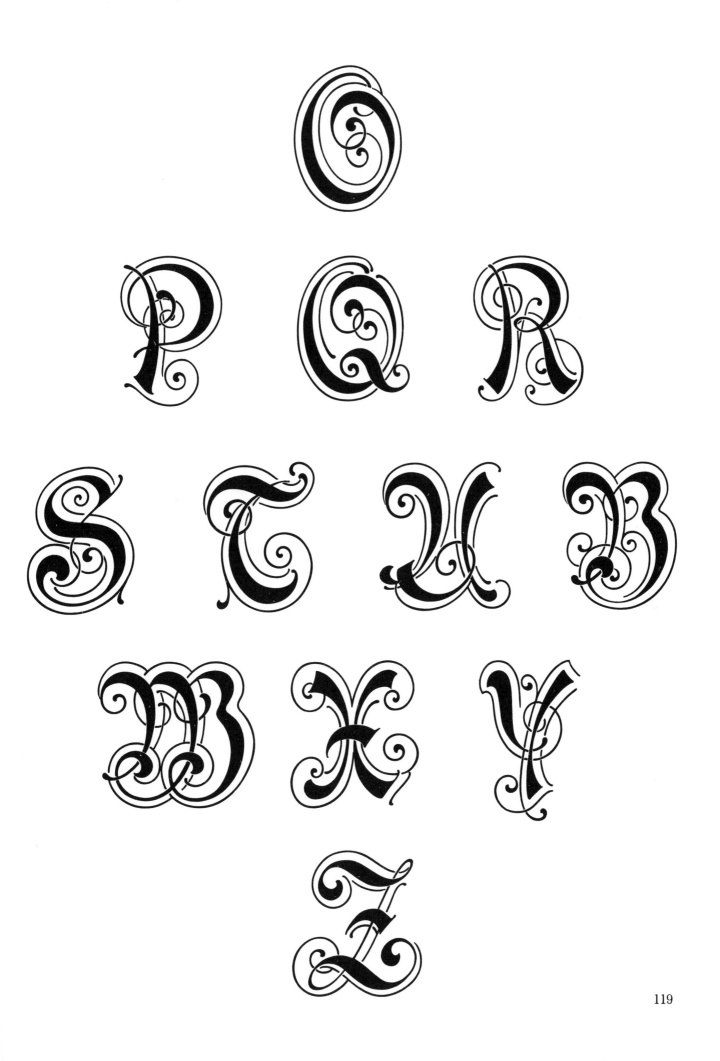

Nn Oo Pp Qq

Rr Ss Tt Uu Vv

Ww Xx Yy Zz